Darling

Darling

HONOR MOORE

Grove Press
New York

Published simultaneously in Canada
Printed in the United States of America

FIRST EDITION

Library of Congress Cataloging-in-Publication Data

Moore, Honor, 1945–
    Darling : poems / by Honor Moore.
    p. cm.
    ISBN 0-8021-3856-X
    I. Title.
    PS3563.O617 D37 2001
    811'.54—dc21   2001035082

DESIGN BY LAURA HAMMOND HOUGH

Grove Press
841 Broadway
New York, NY 10003

01 02 03 04   10 9 8 7 6 5 4 3 2 1

For Inge Morath and Arthur Miller

and to the memory of Paul Schmidt

Contents

Foreword

Houses, certainties, passions—they are lost, in the course of life; it is such losses, in fact, that some poetry acknowledges to be *living*. But as I read through this new book of Honor Moore's, which follows upon *The White Blackbird,* her 1996 account of the painter Margaret Sargent, who was her grandmother; her first book of poems of 1988, accountably titled *Memoir;* and even *Mourning Pictures,* her verse play of 1974, I note with some assurance that the poetic impulse here is not simply to record loss—to mourn and thereby release the energies in us that choose to mourn rather than to founder in melancholy—but also to bear witness, to testify to the truth, to get it down not pat but *right.* I recognize some tonalities of this double impulse from my frequentation of many years— my *audition*—of the painter Lee Krasner, Jackson Pollock's widow, who, in the decades I knew her, was passionately concerned not only with crying the beloved countrymen of the world of art she lived in, but keeping the record straight—on occasion *setting* it straight, knowing herself to be in possession of privileged information. That would be a good title, if she needed an alternative one, for Honor Moore's grave and sorrowing book of illuminations, *Privileged Information:*

> *. . . This is where I measure*
>
> *what I've lost: her voice with its northern*
> *accent speaking my name, my mother*
>
> *close to death, or how my father looks*
> *now, his white hair and crooked teeth.*

The information in such cases *is* the privilege, matter proper to this particular speaker, a *material witness* indeed, and the problem for the poet will be to turn her wan facts into wanton fictions (poems = made things = fictions), toward the accomplishment of which Honor Moore has gathered, indeed has *engendered*, the conventional resources of poetry and then some—overheard voices, the "other harmony" of prose, even the aleatory experiment of "Delinquent Muse," properly to absorb which, Moore teases us, "if you like, read left column, then right, then left to right, as if the break between columns were punctuation or emphasis." Such are the ingenuities and resources of Paulina, explanatory muse of *The Winter's Tale*, who, with exemplary patience, will try any trick, any transition, to bring home her alienated truths to an incredulous tyrant. And it is the case that Honor Moore's revelations are, like Paulina's, more often solacing and luminous than abrupt and painful in Krasner's manner: there is more than one way to skin a catastrophe.

A notable resource—worth noting here for its contribution to the particular loveliness, the lyric aspect, of many of Honor Moore's poems—is the sensuous revelry in which she so generously invites our participation:

> *. . . Standing there*
> *at an ironing board, the dress patterned and torn,*
> *she burns her wrist: and so there will be*
> *evidence. Later, wind and a raw Sunday heat: whites*
> *go whiter, blacks blacken and glare until*
> *eclipsed stripes of blind give actual*
> *seconds of joy: red bougainvillea*
> *late light flushes almost blue, blossoms*
> *folded to the shape of bells so*
> *brilliant now, they seem to tremble and ring out.*

Such are the bonds of experience that in poetry set us free—the wisdom of the senses which assures us that time heals, indeed, by beguiling the body's famous helplessness. It is a felicitous occasion that Honor Moore's new poems— "how almost physical that music"—have become our latest tribulation and relief.

—RICHARD HOWARD

I

Bucharest, 1989

There were other ways that the system used to strangle artistic life. Ms. Undareanu-
Herta said that in recent years it has become increasingly difficult to find oil paints,
and virtually impossible to get hold of the color white.

—*December 31, 1989*
The New York Times

It was white I wanted—of snow, clouds, of sky overcast, of
   a star if you take the shine from it. Usual
      sound, light, and I wake—but sense a shift
of light, a spontaneous tilt in the axis of the sky.
   I cannot tell you what it was that happened
but all day I worked to paint it, no image
      for the change—I needed white.
August and nature past peak. I had fled grief and a city
   where the dark of black had been my modifier:
red turned devilish, green somber, yellow the ocher of walls
      these years of bad coal. I wanted white—
to see what stands around me, to lighten blue
to a sky I can wake up to, of baptism dress,
      bridal gown, candles Christmas—
I could not find it in any shop. There was no announcement
   of this unavailability of white. Could
paint daunt a city plumbed with tunnels? A sentry on each street,
      his face tugged angular, body clad
the moonless starless color of sky the night
they took him from an orphanage cot, taught his hunger
      luxury, his desire to move
a rote of violence. I no longer ask for white. No use writing
   friends or art shops in Paris—just paint white black when

a drift of light recalls candor. They puncture tubes from Paris—
    crimson, cadmium, viridian
    uncoil across the customs desk, turn state
fingers colors I could paint desire. See the glint
        of white on the old man's brow,
his wife behind him hissing assent—a family of tyrants
    with a maggot lust for gold. I turn from gold now,
even the ring my grandmother left. How am I capable
    of this much hatred? White vertical
    cities where our villages were. Cold of
my own embrace this lifetime of unheat. The routine
        balcony panegyric—
a Sunday like any other, then through the crowd something whines
    toward rupture, his arms wild like wash in a storm, his
face as the crowd turns, no guard standing fast, silence from the white
    screen, and then music. Someone will know
    who first shouted, how long it took our breaths to
open with something like emotion, who carried fresh
        oranges from the tunnels, cut a circle
from the center of the flag, who told the first lie.

Courtly Love

A rainbow, where it ends a red MG,
Texas plates, a friend's white empty kitchen.
Out the window a blond stick stretches
blue legs against a red barn door.
I can't see sweat, but her face is red,
hair flaxen, chopped blunt as if a mixing
bowl guided the scissor. Conversation?
Call it awkward. She had run ten miles.

Blood drenches the screen. Lear's sons conspire
on a green mountain. Woman. Knife. More
blood. After, from the car, the moon's slight
scythe doubles in the lake. She wears green
suede boots, speaks an English accent. We are
silent as we drive the length of a night
silver lake. "Thank you," she says. I watch her
cross the dark lot, alight the red MG.

On top of the wood stove, she bakes a cake.
The power has blown. It is a birthday
of mine. She sits in tweed, smoking, argues
down my bad love affair. Freak early snow
douses zinnias. She brings her border
collie, black and white. I spice hot cider.
She doesn't drink either. Always I serve
spaghetti, find later she prefers beef.

She doesn't harangue when I call early.
She tells me a story from her life, paints
blue diamonds across my floor, dog thumping
its tail. The story is about fainting,

a painting, her encounter with a saint.
She asks me to read aloud. Her name means
fate. We drive to her new blue Fox. There is
tenderness in the force of her argument.

I have eye surgery and she cuts
lemons for chicken. In separate chairs
we watch a video about deaf love.
When I drag back from New Orleans, love
lost, she does not argue. The night I drive
north, bearing soup through an ice storm, a sleigh
bed rocks at the edge of a frozen lake.
The dog licks my toes. She kisses first.

In the Dark

It was night that made him strange,
not his gold spectacles or the strained
lay of his skin. Always I say love
before it's strange enough, or strange
at all, but this time, Doctor, I love
our silence, the pale gray stain
his eyes leave in my dreams, the strange
burning of his fingers, strangling
in his long kissing, and the straggle
hope burns, a borealis to strafe
my retinas in the dark. A goat strays
through my dreams, Doctor, a crazy dove,
and from Pontormo, a woman struck
blind, her arms raised against the stranger.

Citizenship

Transvestites bully on the ferry.
Women who once listened won't,
so I can't accomplish what
I've contracted. It's the
terror I want to talk about, sit
in a white room and discuss it.
I don't need a large embrace
or formulaic reassurance
anymore, and the doctor says
cravings for sugar come up
because of sensitivity that's
genetic. Mr. O'Toole, blond hair
slicked, shouts on television.
He keeps saying he's not racist
but it's black people he wants
to exclude, violence engorging
his neck. A black mother gives
her child Comet and Brillo
to remove his graffiti: this
hallway is home. My house is
in the forest. My house
is on a main road. I wake to cars
raging north up a rise, a truck
banging south. Out back deer
gambol, leap the garden fence,
eat my lettuce. It's terror
I want to address, shorn stalks
of chard, lopped bean bushes.

Sleeping Gypsy

I was wearing green. Nineteen.
Flat cheap light illuminates
a male, twenty-one. The female,
a virgin. Him, not. 1963.
Let the light recede. Forget dark
in a red Triumph, street after
midnight, a girl out past the rules.

Or another story: the man who lived
near the lake. Peter, the lifeguard.

Moon over desert. Grand movement of
space. Horizon vanished in the dark.
Our bodies are the bodies of
children, the sky devil-blue, our
desire the color of melon. Words
rattle like keys in a tin. Sex tears
our clothes like a dog at the door.

Her face: for the mouth, a blank.
When she speaks, you can't hear.

My skin is the color of pearl,
edged blue. You move, the past
rippling behind as if you
swim for your life. Green fabric
that does not give. Dreams of
the future spinning like blades.
I would have taken off my clothes.

Or: the man with the curled lip,
burned fingers down between her legs.

Instead I walk from your car
to the tenement. You strut, bastard
Edmund, spotlit. We don't talk.
Others refuse me and I weep
for sentences not made, what lies
behind the ink horizon, a child's
body in the blaze of a cold moon.

Years: then a chance twist back,
the narrow dark of a bright car.

Leaving history: plain light,
a French city that is not Paris.
You say: "Are you in love now?"
What did I wear? The past
bangs, a drunk at the gate.
I hold my ears. Desire again—
a dog leaps through night grass.

Movement: moonlight, a landscape
unlike the bodies of children.

Why has time turned you up,
a trick? I walk from your arms
to the hotel door. In its glass
you bend to your car, a crone.
Had you called out, I would have—
something opens. A crack,
wound of an old silence.

Undertow

She was not cold and I was
still a girl. Okay, I'll never
recover that. She was tall. She
had black hair, her skin tanned fast,
dark blue eyes. I can't remember
her teeth. She liked to wear bright
colors, used the word "sweetie"
ironically. I'll be seventy,
her dead forty-three years, wake
angry and weeping still. She comes
down the stairs wearing black
and white. She comes down the stairs
smiling and the room swerves.
I'm tiny in her arms, as if
flat against a steep mountain.
The sky is strong, pulls at me,
but she holds. Understand, I don't
believe this will ever change.

New Haven, 1969

I remember my body naked—
chalky on a black bear rug,

floor white vinyl tile. Everyone wore
short skirts. He was a student too,

an acquaintance; would like to
photograph me nude. I'm flattered.

Heat of his lights on my skin,
Scotch in two glasses. I don't

remember taking off clothes, just
face and body moving at his

zoom, instructions coming from his
throat. Rain belts at glass, his

lips get wet. When he mounts to shoot
my breasts, his corduroys rub

reptilian on my thighs. He has
a girlfriend whom I like. "Landscape,"

he says. Sets aside Nikon.
Unzips, enters. Ejaculates.

> This happened before the law was changed.
> It's important you know he was not
> handsome, that I was not attracted to him,
> that you know I was thought of

as a good girl even though I had
an older lover, a writer from
New York. I wanted to be a writer.
Short skirts felt embarrassing, but I
loved sex. It's hard to tell the truth. I
wanted to love sex. I was twenty-three.

The gynecologist is bald.
Sun hits his glasses so I can't see

eyes. My breasts are much too hot.
I have money, psychiatrist. He

signs the letter in a room
full of toys. Hospital, stirrups:

if I can't go under, I'll be
a mother. Green mask, instructions

from his throat. I was on the pill,
drunk every night, and lonely.

Often I forgot. Mom said, Don't
come home pregnant. She was pregnant

all the time. Say I missed a day,
two. I could have taken them

religiously. I could have pushed
his fat belly, bent my legs, kicked him

back against the pea-green couch.
I let him kiss, then he rolled off.

    After the law changed, I visited
    a clinic with a friend who worked there—
    a red-haired nurse, red-head daughter pouched
    on her back: procedure rooms painted
    pale blue, a quiet waiting room for
    friends, boyfriends, husbands. "Some women don't
    use birth control or know their bodies
    are their own, so we talk afterward.
    We keep costs down, fees affordable,
    and two of our doctors are women."

A week in bed, the doctor says, or
you may never have a child.

I tell two friends who send flowers.
I tell my lover I am sick,

lie in his tower room, wait.
He stays out late. I remember

the pink dress I wore my first night out.
I began to hurt inside.

I tell him a lie when he wants to
make love. I want to make love.

I tell him the truth and he leaves
for two days. It's an infection.

I call the gynecologist. He
asks if I've told anyone,

prescribes, hangs up. I did not
tell my lover it wasn't his.

I did not tell my mother
or my father. I'm telling you.

Hollow Hill

I am running along the green carpet, away from my
grandmother's bedroom, past the curly maple highboy,
past my father's childhood room where I sleep in his high
bed, to the stairs. My grandfather still walks, so the
elevator has not yet been built. He doesn't talk, and I
have never been allowed into his room, which is not my
grandmother's room, but that is not what I care about
today.

She has given me a doll. My grandmother has given
me a large doll. She has dark hair. She wears a white dotted
swiss dress and the dots are red. She is the most wonderful
doll I have ever had. She is so big she could almost be a
friend. I have left her lying on my father's bed in his old
room. I am staying there rather than in one of the other
rooms because its French door hung with organdy opens
into the hall of mirrors, of mirrored closets, which leads to
my grandmother's bedroom, and my grandmother and I
are alone in the house.

I visit my grandmother after breakfast each morning.
She sits in her canopied bed wearing a pink velvet night
jacket, answering her mail. Her hair is almost white, but
she has a permanent wave that turns it almost blue. A pair
of glasses with transparent frames balances on the end of
her pink nose. As she slashes envelopes with a silver
opener, she talks about Mrs. Roosevelt as if she knows her,
even though she and my grandfather never voted for
Roosevelt. I go to her bathroom which smells sweet, of
lavender and the fumes of her insides. The sink is light
blue. The toilet is light blue. The bathtub is light blue.
There are shepherdesses painted on the blue closet doors,

16

and I am running down the green carpeted hall, green that, if it were blue, you would call slate blue.

I pass the ancestor portraits which stare across at the curly maple highboy. Once my cousin and I found candies in the downstairs bathroom, but no matter how hard I look, I never find them again. I am running down the long green hall toward a mystery. My grandmother says we are alone in the big house, but we are not. The cook is napping. The butler and the parlor maid are napping. The upstairs maid, tall with a beauty mark on her pale cheek but not what I call beautiful, has left for the day. My grandfather dozes in the library. I think of my mother's black hair against her ivory skin, her dark red lipstick against the black of the telephone.

For no reason, my grandmother has given me a doll: the biggest doll I've had. She has dark brown hair, red lips, and brown eyes. The eyes of everyone in my family are blue. My sister must be quite young, my brother still called Pip. I am running along the green carpet. It is a shore or a river and I am a horse. I am a queen whose hair streams as she gallops.

The floors are stained the color of maple. The trees bend in the wind. I run down the hall along the white balustrade, which curves once then descends with the green stairs to the large entrance hall that looks out on the terrace. Or I run to the other end of the hall, all the way to the door of the Modern Room, the room where my parents sleep when they visit, in the only double bed in the house, light from the big windows reflected in its mirror headboard.

They don't let me keep the doll. I gallop back to my father's old room to swoop her up and carry her out on my horse, but she has vanished. There was a phone call, my grandmother says. It isn't Christmas, it isn't my birthday, and so it isn't fair to the other children. I am running down the long hall. The carpet is green. I don't hear the telephone, and I don't hear my grandmother's breathing as I pass out of the hall of mirrors, run to the Modern Room and back. She is the largest and nicest doll I have ever had, but I will never undress her or untie the red ribbons under her chin.

II

Resonance

1.
In the kitchen Sunday morning,
her hand on your shoulder. That's all

you need. A child appears on the bridge,
her gaze follows the child. Your mother

turns, a nurse takes you from her young
arms: night ocean, flare of search,

creatures we aren't meant to see.
Then, night after night, a drench of flu

until you're dreamed free of her
grassy hillside grave. Nothing heals

like that hand. "We don't have a life
together," she says, face toward

the child, window, child running, rush of
lavender across an unpaved bridge.

2.
It was she who wrote twice a week.
You wait in the entrance of the house

where he was a child. Now you are.
Look up! Out French doors, fuchsia

from a canopy of apple tree,
delphiniums reaching, breakfast flowers

gush from Waterford, heliotrope,
bronze child tiptoe in fountain drizzle.

But you stand on red terrazzo.
Is it here the letter reaches you?

It's June, green of everything
possible. It's here the question forms.

One letter of a dozen is his.
When you read it, you always cry.

3.
"The difference between having an idea
and making a cup from clay is

the degree of pain," he says, too tall
for his chair, hands clasped on the table.

What would a life together be?
Fruit spilled, red staining our mouths . . .

I've been lying here wishing
something from sleep—an idea, a shape.

Perhaps he's right about the cup.
You dig the clay or purchase it.

You cover it, keep it wet. One day
the clay calls you to model the cup

and what you've lived, every cup
to your lips, moves through your hands.

4.
His mother is dead now; so is yours.
He's gone white-haired, takes vodka

on a porch by the sea. The big house
is charred, arson its derelict years

up for sale. The gardens? Who knows.
Grape arbor to the roses, smell of

lavender in a thatched herb cottage.
A woman, past, if you're honest,

childbearing, so language won't fall to
my daughter   son   as we walk the bridge.

"A group of little girls," she says, "each
with a toy or color . . ." You turn

to see her mouth open, her teeth
distinct against the color of November.

Double Curse

Each month it happens. I pace
like a fury of Cawdor,
conjure her railing hatred
off somewhere in that blue car.
This is not what I want,
to weep alone, joints dense with
hormonal torque. The sun is
out! blares the window. Sky's bright
blue, but I mourn, Brandenburg
Two proclaiming boisterous
genius in empty rooms. Where
is she? When I look at her
Thursday supper the late half
of a month, her skin is chalk,
mouth priggish against me.
"But I'm innocent!" I shout,
thump fists on the butcher block.
This day last month, I woke
to her eyes-open face and we
fell together like answers.
That was in another country.
Here I curse yellow hair, slim
hips, fierce shoulders. Oh powers
of spring and universe, hear
these gibbous tears! Moon and
goddess, tides and gravity,
Bring our blood! Oh bring our blood!

The Lake

Pale water, mountains almost black, clouds
lifting from the lake—an old dock creaks
at loose moorings and, from the summit, mountains
until the horizon goes blind. What thousand
do you count, walking a narrow bridge
or bending as your canoe glides under it?
This is a language we have written from
always, though it bears its own fate—color
of fern in shade, such a green it must tell
the truth; a thatch of grass points to,
then obscures, underground water; another
tree dead across the path. Compare a sentence
broken as you talk at a table, a gun
in the pocket of a child, the survivor
alone at her desk. She did not teach this—
high heels, gray suit cinched at her waist, red
lipstick, evident jaw. Tell me, how is it
she comes back now? Nor did she teach this—
to hear only one's own voice in the quiet;
or to think alone, out into the dark
pardon of the night. She had no husband,
her hair curled garishly. I can't get back
her voice, just her mouth gesticulating,
and blond Peter who killed himself in London
after we grew up. In the darkness, silent
numbers etch themselves in red. I remember
the pale disk traversed by hands, figures
marking place along a circumference
that lay in wait once, like the future.
In the city night, a door closes—
refrigerator, car, you can't tell which.

What does it mean, she asked us, to be good?
I ask to understand the impulse toward
murder. I ask to be loved. And quiet,
my head between those wide hands, a river
spreads north in autumn light, pale as a lake.
I've seen the beginning of that river,
narrow as a brook, nothing built at its edge.
At the end of the path, a woman turns
to look back, wearing white, holding roses.

Equinox

Heel of hand, fingers, hunger
of animal quickening. All night
eyes see-through as the sea,
body sky in its largeness, cloud
darkening as if for hurricane,
apocalypse, faces agape
as Michelangelo's ceiling
dwellers in the presence of God.

Table laid, candles lit, and the food!
It was a feast—lilies arching
like dancers, the black dog turned
on her back, heat in the floor brick.

Drink as it comes, night rain
of a tropics. Trees beckoning
bituminous green, an aria
of parrots. Oh paint me with clay,
gold, black, blue as a bruise,
but favor the red. And she digs
fistfuls, yield of rock left off
a glacier's rush to the younger sea.

A Window at Key West

Waking in silence and, through tilted blinds,
the mark of red bougainvillea—pink light tossed
at a white door. Out of sleep, I turn
in a narrow bed, and the sheet tugs after me.
Walls the color of milk, wind dragging leaves
across the courtyard, scraping.
Life is incomprehensible, he'd said
when I asked if he had a theory. Late
dalliance of tropical green,
bromeliad, look of palm bark, and beyond

closed windows, a table set for supper.
In my dream I knock. A woman offers spoiled food
then turns away. Now the sky goes dark
and the breeze stops. Why does she ask for narrative?
You make plans but sit instead on a porch
talking about Nietzsche whom you have
never read—never has sense seemed less
consequential. His skin is very black
against the white chair, his voice honest
and loose in the temperate air. The children

ask to walk, but we sink into the large car,
drive the quiet, small streets of an old town. This is
the shape my life takes around absence
any understanding would flatten. Light in the room,
but the sound is blocked—all that suggests it
is movement of light, shadow
rippling a surface of tawny wicker.

There are certain sentences I can't bear
to speak again: *I can love you less.*
Of course I understand. He brings plates of food—

green, then red, yellow. A red biplane, tall
glasses for beer, murmurs near a bar in shadow,
        greeting without handshake or embrace;
then today in a room on the ocean, late silver
light, each chair a distinct bright color. He
        asks only for the present: her face
behind a language I don't speak, something
pulling. Beyond a closed window the noise
        of bodies in water, broken
by the talk of children. Her voice in this room

waylays almost any grief. Standing there
at an ironing board, the dress patterned and torn,
        she burns her wrist: and so there will be
evidence. Later, wind and a raw Sunday heat: whites
go whiter, blacks blacken and glare until
        eclipsed stripes of blind give actual
        seconds of joy: red bougainvillea
late light flushes almost blue, blossoms
        folded to the shape of bells so
brilliant now, they seem to tremble and ring out.

Aubade

Eyes lavender in certain light—today I notice finally. I am looking at your eyes. I am looking at the telephone and you are naked. I have my hands in you and I am thinking of the telephone, cold flat mouth, the day outside. Your hair is the color of raw wood. What's unsaid wheels like the edge of a dead heart. We are all there is, pale as marble, and you are wet and in me moving. Now I know I am frightened and I tell you so. This is the origin of flame, the root of a flower. You have removed my clothes, and we shudder, uncertainty in a climate of faith. When you ask me to open: whales at a tranquil surface, transparency, and movement.

Shoulder

The doctor said tape would keep it from falling apart.
From his table a river falling south, its widening gilt with
sunlight, trees at the near bank. Rough straw-colored tape.
It looked like skin.

I don't know the answer to that question, he said.

It's tiny, an integer of heat or pain, and if I put my arm
behind me suddenly, or if an object resists my hand and
shoves my arm behind me, its force cuts me from daylight.

The path is dark, the trees are wet.

A lake, encircled by mountains. Once I lay down at the
summit of one of those mountains and made love to a
woman. She was enough, I mean she had beautiful skin
and she could open me, but I wanted—

What did you want?
I don't know the answer to that question.
Yes you do.
I wanted the mountain that was under us in me.

Or it comes as a flash of hurt and I want the sky, as if
lightning illuminated the whole sky and the whole sky
stayed bright longer. I want the whole sky.

Let's say the globe breaks at the equator. The half I
want is the half that stays light.

The past is dark, the trees wet, then the moss turns bright as if lit from underneath, and I lie down there. I lie there and wait.

What did the doctor tell you?

It goes out of the heart and into the shoulder. I can feel it, the ligament, but even when I press so it burns, it tells me nothing.

900 megahertz.
I like that word.
It's a good word.
Megahertz.

The path is dark but evident through the trees and the trees are birches. I walk and my shoulder hurts. It's a restraint: I say nothing it won't allow. "Birches are evidence of burning," she says.

The past is ardent. It comes toward me with a serious face, a face so unfamiliar that perhaps it is the future, not the past. I have an illusion I know my past, that we have always been in love, his muscles shining in this kind of light.

Though you can't see how light gets here, there are ferns, like pretty green fur seen under a microscope, fur on a wide skin.

"I don't want to crush them," she says.

A band of white, its underside pink-gold, is peeling from the trunk, languid, its surface pale in the green shady light. Even the table near the window wasn't this vivid. The hurt is a mute question, or possible answers sliding down an upper arm in the guise of pain.

"I'm trying not to fall in love," I tell her.
"Good," she says.

I know I can weep if he says the right word, if he says the right word and I'm leaning against him, against his shoulder. When he stands there, door open behind him to a shiny corridor, the path is evident and quick. The ferns on this ascent describe my ease, of falling, of breaking into him.

The past is dark, the trees wet.

My shoulder is the center of a radiance. When the doctor positions his arms, each beneath each of mine, his chest close behind me, his hands clasped at my sternum, and pulls back sharply, I cry out.

Looking outward, I move through water toward light. The tape that keeps my left arm from moving freely is thick and the color of flesh, but the feel of water replaces pain. To my right is the mountain where I lay on pale grass and made love to a woman. To my left is the mountain whose climb is dense with ferns, pillared with birch. Paper birch that sheds bark like burned skin, whose papery bark flutters, whose paper I strip from its trunk.

I keep the half that stays light.

I like that word.
Which word?

Those morning hours, did my shoulder not hurt or was my heart no longer breaking?

Don't argue with my figure of speech.

What I call heart is radiance, a sky whole and light.

Ravages

An oil fire down below, and on the lit box
an unmoving figure, a man from behind, forearms
bare, walking a path that curves through cared-for
green, each plant placed so unfurling it sculpts
a sort of speech. I breathe with difficulty
and dark rises from the snow. All month
I've been precarious, at a threshold, near
an entrance. No one will say what lies
or what tells the truth. No one can.
If I could, for once, make another visible
this way—outside, cars slice silent air,
and they say the weather's changing.
Last night I heard a man declare with pride
he no longer reads the news—and what they do
they do in our name. Yes, she is beautiful,
like a wide river or an uncomplicated view
of the ocean, but my eyes blank—even
inner vision can't see her now. Such a wide
silence, suddenly I've lost my taste
for spiritual ventriloquy, want to know
just the circling of my own pale hours.
How did this happen again? Nothing happens
again. Eccentricity in her walk, a tilt
as she moves, and I watch as the taxi pulls
south, as she diminishes, the driver's language
nothing I can speak. Every time she's left,
I've let her go without protest, and as
the print of her body leaves mine, ceased
to understand myself. Shoppers interrupted
crossing a street; at the next cut, faces
turned to the wall, blood splashed up stucco;

then the look of wound-scraped skin,
a dying face in bright color. "I stay away
from the news," he says. Frozen rain picks at
window glass and illness sinks through my abdomen.
I'd get an image of your face and long to
fall toward you into touch, just—
A desert, the sickle moon, a black sky
and fire lights her face. Here, light seems to
crack, not extend, and I can't remember
who died yesterday. He was not
old, and he did what I do at the desk,
something beneath his hands to put word to paper.
As we stood there, she pulled me toward her
by the belt and thrust in with her hand.
Tonight cold divides skin from body heat.
What was it like before cars? Before oil burned
in the cellar or jets blanched the sky as if
speed made a difference? In a sunlit room,
I love you more . . . In the kitchen, orange
clivia, its yellow centers, how its broad leaves
shape the light. If I followed her, would I turn
to look back? *We're through half our lives.*
Yes, I answer, as if there were no dead
on certain streets in Europe, no shoppers
hurrying across a square as a wall shudders
from the end of a room—and through a window
you see a face dart forward. On waking,
I beg in the empty dark. Was this a life?
It's the same magenta comforter my sister
carried from Norway as I lay in an oak bed
with a man who loved me, before the telephone

kept memory or screens were linked to language.
It's as if I missed ten or twenty years, certain
lengths of skirt, cuts of jacket. That's where
the Chinese laundry was! I remember the day
I went to say good-bye, the man looking at me
with a fast smile. I was sure I was going somewhere.
Here, from below the fields late at night,
you can hear the train along the river wailing,
wailing hard, between water and the mountains.

Girl in a Fur-Trimmed Dress

Fille à la Fourrure, c. 1889
Henri de Toulouse-Lautrec

It's not a dress, and he hasn't got the lips
right. I'm surprised you sat long enough

that he got you from behind—ostensibly
prim, wearing that orange coat you lied about

losing, which I replaced for you as a gift
and which you sent back to me without a note.

He knew you twenty years before I did—
oh how I fell for you, swooning beneath

those dizzying fingers, green eyes wide
with something I thought more than haste.

We met at a small supper outside Paris
one late August. I wore black, you black

and white. By then your gold hair had gone
off, but I could feel your body. They never

understand that, how a woman's flesh holds
a woman lover long past youth.

He never undressed you or your mouth
would not be open, and you never

looked straight ahead—always your eyes darted,
hungering toward the next enthusiasm.

But he got how you sit, your haunches
holding you down, and clipped you at the hip

to please you, though I suspect those days
you found yourself slim enough to welcome

mouth or finger, had we lain some brothel afternoon
like those whores he's so famous for.

But what you lived long before
put you off any touch, or so I now believe—

the darkened stair, footfalls, another woman.
Surely now your hair has gone dead gray.

I like to think of you looking out windows.
He's got the blue just right and the walls

like bleached fire, orange coat, and creamy
fur encircling your shoulder like meringue.

I am finally now as I was before you
except when I recall—not how you looked

in high middle age or the graze of your hand
but the pitch of your voice—which I turn from

seeking indifference, or a life
whose passions would not have been futile.

Edward

The car, then he moves, opening door suddenly
heavy, farther into the warehouse night, or
perhaps we drive uptown, city darkening, leaving
it all unsaid. You are thinner than ever. We were
children then, really, my fast blue car, a beach,
rooms in which you placed objects with a grace
that flattered God. I was watching men, as you were,
swerving an old car out the dirt drive after
you put guests to bed. On your knees in prayer
now, every day, *fingers at the glands in my neck
like every gay man I know.* Tweed and muffler, beard
patterned across a cheek. *I don't know how
to get past this.* In restaurant dark, friends move
through our conversation as if the past were
a bright street. A mime's fingers. *No one makes
love, and this year there have been so many.*
Oh darling, old friend—of beauty, of exuberant
knowledge—turn as you close the door, take me
as you did then, a bouquet of lilac, a waltz.

Days of rain until you can't remember sun,
breath on the mirror, brothers and sisters
around a New England table. I was hungry
for what you gave, awkward in my largeness:
Delicate, you said, *like a Victorian.*
Offshore, low sound of horns in fog, but the past
comes proudly forward. Who could have told us
it was the present we would find in ruins?
You move across the street like a cello sounding
or like grief—you who travel the places
where the texts were written, cross every floor

like a dancer. There is no wind. I want to hear
your voice, ask how you are. Behind the attic
wall: milk, cookies, late-night talk of book
or film. It's as if someone purposely disturbed
this: a brook runs loud in spring, you live here
with a boy who builds paper castles. I wore
silk, you carried French luggage. Who could see
it was our future we would find in ruins?

Don't be ridiculous! How would I phrase it?
Is your blood poisoned? Or: What is it like
to sit in a beautiful room waiting it out?
There are ten of us here, bent, moving, showing
signs of life, and the sky outside is near gray.
Thursdays, they cut the grass. Either I travel
or stay home. Who are we to each other? I mean,
when you dream figures on a road, am I ever
one of them? You put the key in a car door
then drive a hundred as if we are lovers.
That house: stones painted white, the desert, dust
rising from the driveway, a lizard scuttles up
a whitewashed wall, we dine with a black-haired woman
from Boston. One might argue we knew nothing
of love. Were the trees willows? Yes, and
you showed me plants that grow a hundred years
no matter how dry the ground. What is it I circle
like a plane in weather, or a wooing husband?
You're falling away, darling, aren't you? Slowly.

for Paul Francis Schmidt (1933–1999)

43

Delinquent Muse

heels dug in, and shoulders
skin I must reach for
can't see eyes
or back to desire
what I can't describe
handsome is
the shoulders
he always stands
so light breaks and I see
hand on his hand
splash of flesh at the sleeve
my arms a necklace
for his shoulders
my arms a laughing necklace
heels dug in and leaning
I see the future
at the shore, ocean, a globe
at his cheek
how do you paint a face?
smudged by rain, his
hand at my back
depict what's vanished, shadows
shoulders
how have you—
where have you—
face, its planes articulate
light but the lips, the lips
glass, then eyes
finally again blue
green, looking back
lashes

shape in darkness
washed with music
day through a window
at last it speaks
red of tanager
rising like land
or laughter where
waiting waiting for music
an ocean there
cliff edge slung down
like night, the sun
through a cloud
how do you paint
a face?
here oh come here
so I can see him
in one hand
only once for the kiss
or can you?
face clear across the room
luxury as my eyes
rest at his hairline
and sweep
down the length of him
gone now, inexplicable
feeling, no I'd call it
pain, paint the lips
one after the other
later I could look and
remember early summer
dark slow to come

at an entrance shoulders
in the white room his flesh
the color of a rose
I remember in light
the blue glass, he turns
swear oh swear the question

music into night
a way to understand
what he is
after so much time
toward me now
and the kiss

Hotel Floridia

We are at the beach, Susan carrying her bed.
I have no bed and night is approaching, the water is dark.
Nor do I have appropriate clothes.
All morning I dream what I want, the hot right at my collar breathing.
I can see you don't understand.
I am scaring you.

The sky is teal, the ocean, color of a razor.
A woman carries a butter-yellow umbrella and her
    daughters follow her.

That evening in the city, his hand low on my back, we walked.
When he kissed me on the hotel banquette, he said he
    didn't care.

Ocean the color of a razor.
Once when I was a child, a small child, my father swept his
    long black cloak around me
and we climbed the stone stairs.
Already men were singing
the roof struts meeting like fingers or the inside of a woman.

Susan is carrying her bed.
I have no bed. It's colder.

After he held me that way, he wouldn't talk.
I was the one to turn the shiny knob
shut the door behind him
not watching as he pressed for the elevator.

I open the faucet and water breaks from it
turning pale teal as the tub fills.
Hot is on the left.

It was evening. I could hear men singing across the street
the bell in the tower.

I saw my house collapse, and a man came to the door
with two small children.
He opened the gate and we climbed the stone stairs.
It was cold, so he wrapped me in his long wool cloak which
        was heavy and black.

During the last hour of sleep, Susan beckons me to the
        ocean, an ocean
the color of razor blades for which I am not prepared.
She carries a bed, but I have no bed.
Children race from the sand into the water as the dark rises.
We will sleep here.

At morning sun fills the house so you can see every fault
the chip in shiny white paint
but at evening it is the leaves of ficus you see, grainy in the dark,
evening still giving pale light through the white accordion blind.

"And so," she said, "you come to him quite stripped."
We have been friends for years, and she has watched me.
She has been with me through all of it,
an ocean the color of razors.

You must have been lonely, he said.
I don't know if I was lonely, I said.

When we got near the avenue, we stopped.

All morning you dream what you want, choosing your music.

She Remembers

The Bath, *c. 1895*
Edgar Degas

From a distance, he makes something of me.
Even in the scant light of that darkness

my flesh burns as if his colors were true.
When he finishes, I step into the bath

naked, and he watches me as he has
the others, unspeaking, almost dead-eyed.

What are those behind me? Flowers.
He'd say it doesn't matter what they are,

only what he makes of them. And I break
the water with my left foot, underside

of my right knee slipping down the porcelain
incline, right hand steadied by a towel

slung across the tub's lip. I remember
how dark came, and the radiance of sheets.

My friend accompanied me to Vollard—I hoped
she could keep her face impassive. I wore

a stylish hat like that American woman
he painted once in the Louvre, her arm

long and slender as a closed umbrella.
Should commerce have kept me aloof?

I never was, from the first afternoon
he guided my leg to that angle, and bent

my nakedness until I looked like a jockey
mounting. Afterward, I unbuttoned him

and slid my hand in, pulling with my teeth
at the burnished hair near his shoulder.

We took each other between sheets
he later charcoaled. To the plain wooden bed

and its roil of orange hanging he gave half
the canvas, leaving the shadows for me

to step from air to water, from him
back into myself. I won't say what we did

that I wanted again and again, only
what grief I felt in his wanting, which I see

now in others he painted, women
who come to him, undress for money,

and step in and out of water. My face,
praise God, is barely visible in the sedge

of paint. But I was not ashamed, even when
I lay on the floor and he touched me

with his foot. It was as if we were animals.
Look at the bath. What fills it isn't water

but a wild smudged black, as in the countryside
when night rises, beginning at the ground.

Nocturne

White rose, huge-petaled, blown and bruised
in that stoneware pitcher, and me so young—

a girl who can't know how new she is
but knows spent beauty is an entrance

unfamiliar as her nakedness
after the years without men. His hands

almost, then touch at her waist. I was
about to smooth his hair. Two larches

out a summer window, tomatoes
on a black plate, and beneath the surface

fingers in search of music. "I hate
my hands," he says, and right then I want him

to take me, as instead he holds them
up to the light, as if to make himself

distinct. How almost physical, that
music, that white furniture bruised with us.

The Heron

1.
White city sky, pull of blood down the body,
sleep in which I don't lose consciousness:

a dark-haired woman with a stump for a hand
wades soiled water, stone to stone; whirr

of heat, wallpaper, a hired room; past
doubled glass, white loops of wrought iron,

uptown skyscrapers breaking the clouds.
What replaces loss? A pay telephone, rain,

night, the separate bed, too much salt.
Shift your eyes from the empty chair. Horizon,

path through the woods, a river that flows
upstream, then at the bridge a bright rush of gray.

2.
She was fifty, I suppose, or even younger.
I was five, falling toward her wide soft flank—

though she was not my mother, not that
complicated darkness or thin sallow arm.

Again I dial the number, again busy.
It was afternoon, gray light, her English jarred

by the language of a place where snow
comes early, that the Germans conquered, blond hair

burning to her scalp at an open oven
comes back brown, something about a red dress, how

she met her husband, who was German, uptown.
Take me back to that long afternoon.

3.
My mother and father's bed: outside, a paved
courtyard, broken privet, gate to the street,

the old man with one short leg and high black shoe
muttering Polish; and out of sight, families

whose houses burn in the night, a rat scuffing
tissue near a hole cut to pee through.

She speaks my name as one long vowel, she
teaches me the words for *cheese, thank you,*

as upstairs I lie with her, refusing
love because she works for us and

because her face offers tenderness—simple
as a hand, as ironing a dress.

4.
I walk stubble, water through it like silver
filigree. It is here I have seen

the heron, at a turn in the brook.
This is the hill I climb, this the bridge

I cross, sky I look at. Each time
I wear these clothes: dirt road, then left

into the field, farm equipment rust
in the pasture. This is where I measure

what I've lost: her voice with its northern
accent speaking my name, my mother

close to death, or how my father looks
now, his white hair and crooked teeth.

5.
A black figure on the street passes
a white city wall. Light hangs behind

a silk shade, and a woman tries to comfort
the life I live out long past her death.

A bottle of water on dark polished glass.
I was in my twenties, she was in tears

on the telephone and old. She wanted me
happy, she said. Or was it green silk

that day she met her husband in Yorkville
where you could dance in the afternoon?

The brook turns here and the great bird rises,
wings like the shoulders of a lover.

for Aagot Weickert, 1903–1985

Darling

You came to me one long night in two dreams.
It was the day of your funeral, but you were still alive, vividly
making last-minute arrangements, greeting guests.
The room had the gray shadowy light of a place that has no
    use for day,
but then it opened to sunlight and the walls turned
cream or peach, and there on a platform was a coffin the
    color of chalk
awaiting you. You seemed to wear green, spring green,
    long-sleeved, green-sleeved,
and once in a flash you looked like a woman, as I imagine
    your mother—
dark hair, decisive eyebrows angled in surprise across a
    narrow brow.

Everyone we knew arrived, and people I didn't know,
a great gay poet, old now and tall, with a bright face,
    wearing glasses, a shawl
handwoven of sienna brown wrapped around his head as if
    he were an Arab woman.
You embraced. It was the first time I had seen one man kiss
    another and call him "darling"
and I wondered what had brought you to look at each
    other that way,
to call each other darling here at the edge of death.

Suddenly there is no one in the room, the courtyard
where the coffin is, where the death will take place, no one
    but you and me.

All at once the coffin, which has been floating on water, on
    water faintly blue,
begins to disintegrate, to break apart
like something soluble, and you, in your weakness and illness,
step into the water, which comes to your thigh, and with
    some annoyance,
almost crying at the effort, try to raise it from the water to
    keep it whole.
I watch, and then I am in the water with you, lifting.

I wake from the dream, but in spite of the morning light, I
    am asleep again
and you are there, almost well, turning on the stairs.
As we climb to a large room, I tell you my dream
about the tall gay poet, so old and distinguished in his
    shawl, who embraced you,
whom you held and called darling. Oh yes, you say, with a
    far-off smile
and take me in your arms, lift me and carry me as I protest.
    I don't need
to be carried, you are dying, you'll hurt your back.

You are dressed now, like a servant boy in tattered
linens, as if costumed for a play.

Dear one, I have met a man who touches me so it burns.
I am wearing beautiful pale clothes, and we are standing in
    a room, my hands open as he
feels at the length of me, as he looks seriously into my face,
    or down

my body, his hand holding the place between my legs,
        waiting there or
questioning, as I burn down into his fingers, my arms
loosening, whoever I am sheared away.

I tell you this even though I'm not sure what you'll say back.
In life you might have shrugged, keeping quiet
all those years of sex, what happened those nights you left
        after dinner
before you got sober, before the disease came that took
        you and all your friends
and with them, a certain languor and handsomeness.
I imagine that in death whatever kept our silence may have broken,
that you might now understand what this man's hands
        force me to question
how far desire takes the body before mindfulness leaves it,
what it was for you when a man's touch
burned you open, or burned you back to such blankness
        and hope
there was nothing you wouldn't do to have him.

Mazurka

The same gray lasts through a whole day until
sometimes at evening when clouds part and a piece of
harsh light falls through. I remember this and the river at
night. When I lived here, all that time ago, I stood once at
a window high above the city and watched ice pass below,
chunks of it, on this river. Now the water flows all year: in
sunlight that sharp blue; under this gray sky, the color of
greased steel.

I walk the park in the morning, trees rising from
packed earth, the seduction of snow offered, then quickly
withdrawn. Along the river, down city blocks—beneath the
reckless din of the city lies something more like a body. I
can't keep from the building where he lives, brick like the
others but close to orange in color, a curve along the river.
In the pale room I listen to music, the old dead Russian
playing mazurkas. I remember a room of girls wearing
white dresses and dancing mazurkas the length of a long
bright floor, out tall windows that gray light. I am not
interested in this sentence: *I am older now.* Or in this one:
I am no longer young. The pictures on the wall here do not
belong to me: a boy in charcoal, a few French landscapes in
crumbling gilt frames. I can't keep from walking past his
door, dark tile floor, a rubber mat across it to protect from
the snow, elevators, a list of names in white letters. I think
of the dim colors of winter coats, my face turned so a cheek
or forehead catches the light: you are smiling, believing in
the future. It would have seemed normal to accept a
bouquet, as if I understood flowers, the shapes of them. As
I walk, my long skirt looks like black petals upside down,
and your hand is at my back.

This morning it was mild, like spring. Now it's cold. When I lived here, I rarely thought of this city as an island, but it is one, set where a great river opens to the Atlantic, so the weather is changeable as weather is near the sea. A workman in the elevator bends to stroke my dog.

His voice was neutral until I said my name. "Would you like to have lunch sometime?" I have been falling in love since I was a child. *Neutral* means the shoulders hunched, the gait slow, the eyes barely seeing. *Particular* means I distinguish color, walk quickly, speak to strangers, laugh at everything. This was not to be a story, rather a meditation on returning to live in the city of her birth, the city where she went to school as a young girl, where her friend danced the mazurka, the city into which her parents disappeared a night each week, leaving her in a dark narrow house with her little brother and two sisters and a woman from Norway. It was to this city that she returned as a young woman, in this city that she became a woman, if making love with a man makes one a woman, if making love to another woman can be said to make one a woman.

In those years, she drove north along the river as the sun fell, day darkened, and the water brightened until it looked like a blue opal. Now the ground of her dreams breaks beneath her night after night, like clouds pulling apart at the end of a day to let through that crash of new light. It was summer, the crowd dressed in light colors, she waited for him to return. He pointed at two men accidentally dressed alike, and she laughed. He asked when her birthday was, and she told him. They left quickly because the sky was white and it was terribly hot. He drove the long narrow road as they told each other stories. Green grass, green distance, green leaves.

At lunch they remember none of this. They greet each other, climb stairs to the dining room, sit across from each other. They converse. She wears a dull green jacket, the scarf at her neck black with a streak of green, sits with her arms folded on the lip of their table. She watches his face which is the same face, though up close now she can see every hour of their separation imprinted on his skin. Dear, dear face. And then the storm breaks, suddenly as if in the tropics, palm trees twisting, green turning gray, leaves flying off like wings, sky almost yellow in the strange light. It is an ordinary story of pasts unfinished or of misunderstanding. Do you want to hear it?

None of it seems relevant when they first meet, she in that red coat, he at the stove stirring as she washes the salad. So long ago now! They can't keep from smiling, his skin is so smooth, clear and new. "You're just a baby," he exclaims when she tells him her age. "Have you enjoyed your lunch, sir?" The old black man bows at the edge of the table, linen towel slung from his forearm. Remember that night in the meadow behind your house? The windows were gold behind us in the dark, and the others had gone down to the pond. You went back to the house to adjust the light, and I waited for you, and then we sauntered to the water's edge, your hand at my back. Now the storm uproots even the light, leaving its mark on his skin, taking even memory. I didn't want to leave you, but you raised black wings, as if we had never recognized each other, never kissed or opened our mouths in the dark.

"You fell in love with him, but he didn't fall in love with you," she said. We were eating lunch in a bright room, food spread out on a glass table, and I was telling her the story. Don't ever tell your story. Keep it to yourself.

Does he have a story that begins with *my* skin? With his hand, weighted like a blossom with rain, grazing my cheek that early evening, water rushing far below? This was not to be a story, but a meditation on her return to the city. He hands her a menu which she glances at. He writes what she wants, what he wants. Before the storm breaks, he finishes his food. She can barely eat. "Was it all right?" he asks her. She drinks cold tea as men begin to rake in the storm debris. She was not hungry. Afterward, they rise from the table. Daily life should not have allowed that walk down the stairs, coats, a street lit by that same gray light. She stands there and he extends his hand. "Good-bye," he says through a small mouth.

She wore a black scarf with a streak of green. It was new and made in Paris. Stiffened silk, pulled into a jaunty bow. She kept looking at his face, looking for something she recognized, something to return her gaze. The same gray light through a whole day until sometimes at evening when clouds part and a piece of harsh light falls through. She remembers this and the river at night. His voice will never be green again, she thinks, and writes it down.

Notes

Courtly Love
Lear's sons: In *Ran*, Akira Kurosawa's film version of
Shakespeare's play, King Lear has sons rather than daughters.

In the Dark
Jacopo da Pontormo, 1494–1556, Italian Mannerist painter.

Sleeping Gypsy
Edmund was the illegitimate son of Gloucester, in *King Lear*.

Double Curse
Cawdor
"Thane of Cawdor"—Macbeth, in *Macbeth*.

Girl in a Fur-Trimmed Dress
Henri de Toulouse-Lautrec, *Fille à la Fourrure*, c. 1889–1891, study
for *Au Moulin de la Galette, Peinture à l'essence* on cardboard,
Private Collection, Switzerland.

Delinquent Muse
If you like, read left column, then right, then left to right as if the
break between columns were punctuation or emphasis.

She Remembers
Edgar Degas, *The Bath*, c. 1895, oil on canvas, The Carnegie
Museum of Art, Pittsburgh.

"Vollard": Ambroise Vollard, one of Degas's dealers, purchased
the painting from Degas's estate after his death. For the purposes
of the poem, I imagine the painting hung for a while in his Paris
gallery.

". . . that American woman": Degas painted Mary Cassatt at the
Louvre, balancing her hand on a closed umbrella.

Acknowledgments

My utmost thanks to Forrest Gander, Andrew Wylie, Sarah Chalfant, Jeff Posternak, and Sonesh Chainani; and at Grove Press, especially to Joan Bingham, Hillery Stone, Charles Woods, and Muriel Jorgensen. Thanks also to Joan Larkin, Carolyn Forché, Alfred Corn, Stanley Siegel, Kennedy Fraser, Marguerite Whitney and Tom Whitney for Key West, Adriana Timus for Bucharest, John D'Agata, C. D. Wright, Virginia Anstett, Alison Rose, and to my students, who give more than they know.

Grateful acknowledgment is made to the publications that first published these poems:
American Poetry Review: Citizenship, Undertow
The American Voice: Hollow Hill
Caprice: Resonance
Columbia: New Haven, 1969
Conjunctions: Delinquent Muse, The Lake, Hotel Floridia, Darling
Kunapipi (UK): The Lake, Girl in a Fur-Trimmed Dress
Open City: She Remembers, The Heron
The Paris Review: Bucharest, 1989, A Window at Key West, In The Dark (as Strange Love)
Ploughshares: Courtly Love, Sleeping Gypsy
Salmagundi: Nocturne, Double Curse
The Seneca Review: Shoulder, Mazurka
Slate: Edward
Tikkun: Ravages
Yellow Silk: Equinox, Aubade